Dog Breeds: Profiles of Popular Dog Breeds and Buying Advice

Troy Ludo

Published by Troy Ludo, 2022.

DOG BREEDS: PROFILES OF POPULAR DOG BREEDS AND BUYING ADVICE

First edition. December 24, 2022.

Copyright © 2022 Troy Ludo.

ISBN: 979-8215778258

Written by Troy Ludo.

Also by Troy Ludo

Aquarium Care Made Simple
How To Lose Weight: And Stay In Shape Permanently
Easy Self Improvement: The Ultimate Guide
Dog Breeds: Profiles of Popular Dog Breeds and Buying Advice
Single Parenting: Become Your Child's Best Parent!

Dog Breeds: Profiles of Popular Dog Breeds and Buying Advice

Topics Included:

Introduction

Do You Need a Golden Retriever as Your Pet?

You want a Collie, right?

Are Labrador Retrievers a Good Fit for You?

Do You Want a Cocker Spaniel?

You'd like a German Shepherd, then

You'd Like a Bulldog, Right?

Do you belong to the Boxer breed?

Does a Basset Hound Fit Your Lifestyle?

You say you want a Beagle.

Do You Want a Chow Chow as a Breed?

Do You Want a Yorkshire Terrier?

Do You Want a Boston Terrier?

Does a Rottweiler Fit Your Personality?

You say you want a Dalmatian.

Does a Doberman Pinscher Fit Your Lifestyle?

Dog Breeds: Profiles of Popular Dog Breeds and Buying Advice

Introduction

Looking for a new furry friend? You're in luck! This guide provides profiles of popular dog breeds, along with breed-specific buying advice. From Bloodhounds to Yorkshire Terriers, there's a perfect pup out there for everyone. So what are you waiting for? Start reading and find your four-legged soulmate today!

Do You Need a Golden Retriever as Your Pet?

After reading THE WATCHER a dozen times and witnessing Golden Retrievers in action as guide dogs, you now want to get a Golden Retriever puppy of your own. However, you must be certain that a Golden Retriever is actually the best dog for you and your family before bringing one of these adorable yellow fuzzy balls home.

The Golden Retriever is a large, powerful dog with a shoulder height of 21 1/2 to 24 inches and a weight range of 55 to 75 pounds. It's possible that the large cranium of this dog breed contributes to the intelligence of Golden Retrievers.

The hues of the coats range from a dark, honey-colored gold to a pale, almost-white gold. Any white splotches or marks, as well as the lightest or deepest shades of gold, are seen to be undesirable.

In the beginning, Golden Retrievers were bred to be working dogs, did you know that? Members of the Sporting Group, they are. These dogs are energetic creatures that require a lot of activity, especially while they are younger than three years old.

One reason why Golden Retrievers make good search and rescue, Seeing Eye, or narcotics detection dogs is their willingness to be occupied. If you don't keep them busy, they'll find other methods to amuse themselves, like chewing all of your shoes.

Since most Golden Retrievers love to dig, if you are an ardent gardener, you need make sure you have a separate area where you can keep your dog. They are also prone to chewing up plants when they are in their puppy stage.

Given that Golden Retrievers are large dogs, you might want to think about how much food will cost before getting one as a puppy. They consume a lot of food. Additionally, considering that Golden

4

Retrievers are susceptible to hip dysplasia, you might want to talk to your vet about giving your puppy food that is specifically designed to promote healthy growth in big breed puppies.

You might need to think about whether a Golden Retriever puppy will be too rambunctious for your young children if you have any. Goldens are great family dogs as adults, but puppies can be rather mouthy and unruly. While playing, they could unintentionally knock toddlers to the ground.

If you do decide to purchase a puppy while you have young children, you will need to immediately find the time to teach him manners.

To help him become acquainted to other dogs and people and to learn how to behave when he is outside the house, you might wish to take him to obedience courses. It's a good idea to train your puppy before he becomes too strong for you to simply control.

To prevent their coats from tangling, Golden Retrievers require routine maintenance. Given its propensity to grow thick mats, the area behind your dog's ears needs specific attention.

When your dog is shedding, there may be a lot of dog hair on your furniture. Regular grooming will help you reduce this. The time needed to examine your dog for ticks after a frolic in the park or other grassy and wooded places is also necessary.

5

If you're still convinced that this is the breed for you, make sure the breeder you choose to purchase your puppy from is reputable. A Golden Retriever in good health and temperament is a delightful, wise companion.

You want a Collie, right?

Nearly all kids desire to own Lassie, the magic Collie.

Unfortunately, a Collie puppy could come as a bit of a letdown if the child really hopes for one dog to be so amazing. After all, countless devoted Collies perform the role of Lassie in real life.

The Collie breed is a great option for a family dog because it was developed to herd sheep and still possesses a strong protective instinct. Of course, not all Collie breeds make excellent watchdogs.

While some of these dogs are anxious and high strung, the majority get along great with kids. The Collie is categorised as belonging to the herding group by the American Kennel Club. These dogs are 22 to 26 inches height and 55 to 80 pounds.

The Collie is a powerful, elegant dog with a lot of endurance. Whether they are brown or blue, this dog's almond-shaped eyes seem to glitter with intelligence. The Collie has prick ears that provide the impression of alertness.

The Collie's coat can be either rough or smooth. A smooth coat is shorter and less full than a rough coat. This breed is available in blue merle, tricolour, or sable and white.

The Collie appreciates being close to a busy household. Due to its love of being outside, this breed is not suitable for apartment living. The Collie breed thrives in a house with a sizable yard.

The Collie is a pleasant and gregarious dog, but it also protects its family and is serious about its job as a watchdog. Regardless of whether they are people, cats, squirrels, or pieces of trash blowing around the yard, your Collie will bark at intruders.

As a puppy, the Collie may be pretty brazen and get into lots of trouble. You should think about enrolling your Collie in puppy obedience courses because it is simpler to train a little puppy without bad habits than a sixty-pound dog with them.

Also, if you don't want Collie hair on every piece of furniture in your house, be sure to be strict with your puppy about keeping on the floor. Once you've given your dog permission to sit on the furniture, he'll think he has a right to do so whenever you leave the room.

7

There are not many health issues with the Collie breed. The most frequent issues these dogs encounter are eye conditions and PRA. In fact, you are much more likely to take your dog to the doctor for an injury sustained when he was jumping from a moving car or while he was sauntering around than you are for a medical issue.

Collies are more than glad to store a lot of food. It is preferable to offer these dogs three little meals a day because they have a propensity to overeat. Consult your veterinarian about switching to a meal that encourages weight loss if your Collie begins to develop a bulge around his middle.

Even though a rough-coated Collie has lengthy hair, little care is required. In order to prevent mats, go over your dog's coat many times a week, paying special attention to the hair on his face, in back of his ears, and on his legs.

The Collie is a well-educated household pet. The Collie can be the ideal companion for you if you want a dog that would play with the kids and guard your family.

8

Are Labrador Retrievers a Good Fit for You?

Consider getting a Labrador Retriever if you want a dog with a pleasant disposition and a strong desire to make you happy. Of course, not everyone will enjoy these large, boisterous canines.

Consider some of the breed's benefits and drawbacks before purchasing one of these roly-poly tiny puppies.

The Labrador Retriever is a strong, trustworthy canine. This breed stands between 21 and 24 1/2 inches tall at the shoulder and weighs between 55 and 80 pounds. These dogs can work or play for long periods of time since they have a lot of stamina.

The large, rounded tail and velvety, chocolate-brown eyes of labs are their trademark features. The most widely accessible Labs have black coats, though they can also have yellow, chocolate, or other colours. The Labrador Retriever's coat is made up of dense hair that is practically waterproof.

9

The American Kennel Club categorises Labrador Retrievers as belonging to the Sporting Group. These dogs were developed to spend hours locating game in difficult-to-access places. Labs are frequently fond of the water, making them excellent boating or fishing companions.

Particularly when they are young and energetic, these dogs need a lot of exercise. They don't make good apartment dogs because they need lots of space to play and run around.

The optimum setting for a Lab is a house with a fenced yard. Even if he has room to play, he might still need to take daily walks or run around in the park to get some energy out.

Because they have a lot of muscle and are high energy dogs, Labrador Retrievers consume a lot of food.

You might wish to give your puppy food that is specially developed to support the development of strong bones in large breed dogs while it is still a puppy. You must get dog food that is high in protein if you intend to utilise your Lab as a hunting dog.

The majority of Labrador Retrievers are wonderful family pets and adore kids. If as all possible, see both parents before purchasing a puppy because some Labs do not have nice temperaments.

If your kids are young, you might want to hold off on getting a Lab dog until they can stand unassisted. These canines have such strong tails that they can easily topple young children.

10

It's crucial to begin teaching your puppy between the ages of eight and twelve weeks due to the size of labs. A fully grown Lab can knock people over with an eager greeting, so make sure you train with your puppy to prevent it from jumping up.

Given that Labs can occasionally be a little headstrong, you might want to enrol him in puppy obedience classes to socialise him and obtain some training assistance.

Almost no grooming is required for Labrador Retrievers. To get rid of loose hair and grime, you want to brush your dog once every week.

Additionally, when his nails become too long, you will need to cut them. Finally, once your dog has played outside, you must check for ticks.

A Labrador Retriever can be the ideal breed for you if you want a pleasant dog who is eager to please and don't mind some sporadic stubbornness.

11

Do You Want a Cocker Spaniel?

It is challenging to realise that the Cocker Spaniel was originally bred to be a working dog because this breed exhibits such beauty and grace in the show ring.

However, Cocker Spaniels were intended to work hard with hunters and sportsmen before they were bred for their long, flowing coats.

The spirited little Cocker has lost much of its prior hunting instincts nowadays. Instead, keeping this breed as a family pet has grown in popularity.

Cocker Spaniels are little canines that weigh between 24 and 29 pounds. They have a height of fifteen to sixteen inches. This type is distinguished by its floppy ears, long, feathery leg hair, and dark, deep eyes.

Black, cream, roan, black and white, orange and white, tan tricolour, and black with tan points are just a few of the many hues available for the Cocker.

Cocker Spaniels were so well-liked for a while that some breeders permitted unruly dogs to procreate. The offspring with undesirable traits were bred to other canines with undesirable traits.

The Cocker Spaniel breed was suddenly overrun with dogs that had uncontrollable fits of fury or were exceedingly sensitive. Fortunately, breed enthusiasts intervened to save the breed and have been producing puppies with good temperaments ever since.

The majority of Cockers are once again excellent family pets and get along well with kids and other animals. Make sure you only purchase from a reputable breeder and see both parents if you want to ensure that the Cocker Spaniel you buy has a nice disposition.

Cocker Spaniels adapt well to living in apartments, townhouses, or single-family homes because they are low-energy dogs. Your dog will still require daily exercise, though. Your Cocker will be overjoyed if you have a kid who enjoys throwing balls or sticks because these dogs like the game of fetch.

It is still a good idea to teach your dog, even though Cocker Spaniels are tiny enough to be readily controlled when they are fully grown. He will learn how to get along with people and other dogs at puppy lessons.

Since owners are truly learning alongside their dogs in these programmes, they are also a good concept for new dog owners.

13

A good bit of care is necessary for the Cocker Spaniel's coat, especially if you want your dog to have those gorgeous feathery leg hairs.

Be ready to brush your Cocker's coat at least three times per week if you don't maintain it short-cropped. Keep a close eye on your dog's ears because they frequently don't receive enough airflow to stay healthy.

Cocker Spaniels are known for being somewhat gluttons. Make sure you feed your dog in the right portions. Additionally, you might want to think twice before using sweets as training incentives.

In addition to obesity, the attractive Cocker can experience various medical issues. Hip dysplasia, damaged knees, epilepsy, vision issues, heart disease, and allergy issues are a few of them.

A Cocker Spaniel can be the ideal breed for you if you're looking for a little family dog with a playful nature.

14

You'd like a German Shepherd, then

The German Shepherd has developed from an already well-known dog breed to one of the most well-known breeds on earth ever since Rin Tin Tin rose to fame as a popular television personality.

This adaptable canine breed appears to be everywhere where a dog can be helpful, from nations that are embroiled in conflict to regions that have just experienced natural disasters. The strong German Shepherd will terrorise criminals one moment and put up with the overly cuddly attention of young children the next.

German Shepherds are still quite protective by nature because they were bred to be guardians. It is never a good idea to breed a nervous or high strung dog because the offspring may turn out to be unreliable.

However, the majority of German Shepherds make fantastic pets who are devoted to their families—including kids and other animals—in every way.

15

The German Shepherd is a medium-sized dog that can reach heights of twenty-two to twenty-six inches and weighs between sixty and seventy pounds. This breed has beautiful ears, dark, perceptive eyes, and erect ears.

German Shepherds are most frequently black and tan, but they can also be black and grey or grey and tan. An Alsatian is a striking all-white dog that is well-liked by many people.

If the Alsatian breed appeals to you, make sure you meet the parents of the puppy because these white German Shepherds can occasionally be a little high strung.

German Shepherds are energetic animals, although they can live in urban areas. Just keep in mind that your dog will need frequent exercise and that he will be unhappy if you leave him unattended for a prolonged period of time without providing him something to do. Of course, the ideal home is one in a rural region with a sizable yard.

You might want to sign your German Shepherd puppy up for obedience training when he's a puppy because he'll grow into a big, strong dog very quickly. A little puppy is considerably simpler to handle than a large, untrained dog.

Puppy obedience training also aid in your German Shepherd puppy's socialisation with other dogs and people, which is another crucial benefit.

16

The regrettable misconception that these intelligent dogs need to be trained as security dogs is one that many dog owners share.

However, if your dog is not properly trained, this training could result in aggressiveness. German Shepherds do not require attack dog training to guard your home because they are inherently protective.

The German Shepherd's coat doesn't require much maintenance. The coarse, dense coat is dense and resists matting. To get rid of dirt and other debris, brush your dog once every week.

Concrete will undoubtedly break your Shepherd's nails if you live in a city. In contrast, if your dog lives in a rural region, he can require nail trimming on numerous occasions a year.

German Shepherds require a nutritious diet made specifically for large size dogs. You might need to give your Shepherd a high-protein diet if he is a working dog. A excellent dog vitamin is another wise choice.

Hip dysplasia and epilepsy are typical ailments in this devoted, intelligent breed. It is heartbreaking to watch one of these noble canines afflicted with any condition. Make sure the parents of your puppy have been tested by the breeder to make sure they don't have these diseases.

A German Shepherd can be the best dog for you and your family if you want a canine companion who will be devoted and protective.

You'd Like a Bulldog, Right?

Bulldogs are much more than just a dog with sad eyes and droopy jaws, although their appearance is one of the main factors in their appeal. The fact that these dogs are docile and sweet-natured is another factor contributing to their popularity.

This breed was initially developed to aid in the slaughter of bulls by butchers. Some individuals trained their dogs to goad bulls by using the bulldog's tenacity.

People who loved the breed started breeding only the most affectionate dogs when this nasty sport was made illegal. These dogs are now gregarious, amiable creatures.

Despite being a medium-sized dog, the bulldog is nonetheless incredibly strong. These dogs are 12 to 16 inches tall and weigh 40 to 50 pounds. A bulldog has a flat forehead, broad jaws, and a squat physique. These dogs have soft, dark eyes. Bulldogs can have straight tails or corkscrew tails, depending on the breed.

18

This breed is categorised as a part of the Non-Sporting Group by the American Kennel Club. These peculiar-looking dogs just exist to be loyal pals. Fortunately, they are perfectly suited for the job.

The best pets for apartment dwellers are bulldogs. They don't need to spend a lot of time exercising because they have very little energy. Of course, they still take their owners on lengthy evening walks.

Of course, the Bulldog has some shortcomings, just like every breed. Because this species commonly snores, drools, and passes gas, living with one can make you feel like you are in a frat house. One of these often affectionate dogs will occasionally bully other dogs, especially if food is involved.

Bulldogs, despite their small size, have a lot of strength. As a result, it will be much simpler for you to begin teaching your dog when he or she is a puppy.

Fortunately, even if they are not always quick learners, these dogs are anxious to please their owners. Even the most basic orders might be difficult for young Bulldogs until they are six months old.

A bulldog is known for being a bit of a chow hound. This breed enjoys food. But because obesity may cause major health issues, you must be careful not to let your Bulldog overeat. Allergies, hip dysplasia, eye, respiratory, and other health issues also affect these con artists.

19

Owners of bulldogs must take extra care to keep their canines out of the sun. These canines are prone to heat stroke, which can be fatal.

Additionally, as this breed is susceptible to breathing issues, choke collars should never be used when walking Bulldogs. You can protect their tracheas, which are already little, by using a harness.

Bulldogs have short coats and require relatively little care. However, they need to carefully wipe their facial creases. Your Bulldog risked getting skin diseases, in addition to developing an unpleasant odour, if you neglected to keep his wrinkles clean.

A bulldog can be the ideal breed for you if you want a devoted family pet and are willing to overlook the fact that your little guy has a tendency to stink a little bit.

Do you belong to the Boxer breed?

You might wish to look at the Boxer if you want a dog that is kind with kids but a potent deterrent to crooks. The Boxer got its name because when it fights, it has a habit of boxing with its front legs.

20

These strong canines were initially employed as hunting dogs, but they quickly gained popularity in Europe as police and military dogs. Boxers became popular as companion dogs as soon as people saw how devoted and caring they were to their family.

Oddly enough, it wasn't until men returning from World War II with some of these dogs that the adaptable Boxer gained popularity in the United States.

Despite being categorised as medium-sized canines, boxers are as strong as large dogs. A young, healthy boxer weighs between fifty and eighty pounds and is full of muscle and energy.

These dogs resemble bulldogs in appearance, with broad chests, thick skulls, and broad faces. These canines are not beyond using a mournful "poor me" attitude to get their way, and their huge brown eyes are quite expressive.

Boxers should have black mask-like markings on their faces and be fawn or brindle in colour. White markings on a dog are seen as showy.

A Boxer will not be permitted to compete in the show ring if more than one-third of its body is covered in white or if it is all white. In addition, white Boxers are more likely to develop hearing and other health issues.

21

A Boxer might not be the best breed for someone who lives in an apartment. These dogs need to be able to exercise frequently because they are high energy creatures.

A Boxer would thrive in a home with a properly secured yard. A Boxer can quickly jump over smaller fences, so you'll need to make sure the fence is high and sturdy enough to keep your dog in.

Even while most Boxers get along well with other dogs, if you already have a small dog or cat, you might not want to purchase a Boxer. If you do have other dogs, you might want to think about neutering your Boxer around six months to control their hostility.

Boxers get along well with young kids, yet until he grows, he might be too bouncy to play with toddlers. After all, an excessively enthusiastic welcome from a young, excited Boxer might easily knock an adult to the ground.

Boxers need to be enrolled in obedience training while they are still manageable due to their high level of energy and power. You may socialise your Boxer and teach him how to get along with other dogs by enrolling him in puppy classes.

These dogs should pick up simple obedience commands easily because they have a strong desire to please. You might want to give your Boxer advanced obedience and agility training as well.

22

Boxers don't need much grooming. To prevent having to vacuum pet hair off of the floor, simply brush through your dog's sleek coat once a week to remove any loose hair. Additionally, you should brush your dog's teeth and examine his nails to see if they require trimming.

Boxers have large appetites. Given that Boxers are prone to hip dysplasia, you should think about giving your dog a meal designed for large dogs. There aren't many other major health issues that these dogs have. Before purchasing a puppy, you may wish to inquire about a family history of thyroid or heart issues.

So, if you're looking for a dog that will be a loyal friend and companion, a Boxer can be the best breed for you.

Does a Basset Hound Fit Your Lifestyle?

You might find it difficult to resist getting a Basset Hound puppy if you melt at the sight of large mournful eyes. These canines have beautiful, caring personalities on top of eyes that could melt even the hardest hearts.

23

With its sharp nose, the Basset Hound can detect smells almost as well as its forebear, the Bloodhound.

In fact, this member of the hound group of the American Kennel Club is likely to get so fixated on a scent that he will disobey orders to come or heel. In order to trace odours in confined spaces where larger scent hounds could not fit, Basset Hounds were developed.

The Basset Hound is about eighteen and twenty inches tall and weighs about sixty pounds. These dogs can be any of the AKC-recognized hound dog colours, but the most typical coloration is a white base coat with brown and black patches.

The Basset has long, floppy ears that, when he is standing, almost touch the ground. Although he appears goofy and ungainly due to his undershot jaw, thick chest, and small legs, this dog can move quite beautifully.

As long as the surrounding neighbours don't mind their sombre vocalisations, Basset Hounds are excellent apartment dogs. These dogs actually don't enjoy exercising unless they're searching for a smell, but they need to exercise every day for their health.

Even if your yard is fenced in, you still need to go for walks with your Basset to keep him in shape.

A Basset Hound is a great choice if you're seeking for a pet that gets along with kids and other animals. These canines like people and will go to any lengths to be with them.

24

For the sake of being able to spend time with the kids he adores, more than one Basset has faced the humiliation of dressing up in frilly robes.

Basset Hounds are affectionate and dedicated companions, although they may be stubborn at times. Some individuals believe their Basset isn't intelligent enough to learn obedience because of this stubbornness and believe it is a fault with their intelligence.

But if you pay close attention to your Basset when he disobeys, you could just notice a mischievous sparkle in his huge, mournful eyes. In contrast to directions that don't interest him, like the stay command, your Basset is more likely to follow instructions that indicate he will be spending time with you.

These dogs might be a little challenging to teach, so you might want to think about enrolling your puppy in obedience courses to obtain guidance from a trainer.

The Basset Hounds enjoy eating. You must closely monitor your Basset's food intake because of their chow hounding tendencies and lack of interest in exercise. Ask your veterinarian to suggest a meal that will help your Basset shed weight if he gets too fat.

Bassets don't need much grooming. Once a week, he gives his hair a brushing to get rid of grime and stray hairs. As the air may not flow efficiently in such droopy ears, you may also need to examine his ears to ensure he doesn't develop any issues.

25

In fact, one of the biggest health issues with this breed is ear infections. Eye illnesses and damage to the spine are two other major health issues.

A Basset Hound can be the ideal pet for you and your family if you desire a dog whose only goal is to please his people.

You say you want a Beagle.

A group of these little dogs running after a fox or a rabbit while barking at the top of their lungs is usually what comes to mind when you think about Beagles. Despite the fact that these dogs have been used for hunting for many centuries, they can make fantastic household pets.

The Beagle has a keen nose and a powerful instinct for hunting. There are two sizes available for this hound group member of the American Kennel Club: under thirteen inches and thirteen to fifteen inches. The only difference between the two breeds of Beagle is size.

26

The beagle has a long tail, floppy ears, and dark eyes. Its short, mostly tan, black, and white coloured coat is characteristic of the species. There are other canines that are orange, black, or brown with white markings.

The Beagle can adjust to apartment living, but if he repeatedly alerts you to unexpected noises, he can end up disturbing your neighbours. You must take your Beagle for long walks or take it for a romp in the park since these dogs need to burn off some of their constant hunting energy.

However, be cautious before letting him go off-leash because a Beagle who is hard on the trail of a rabbit will forget everything he learned about obedience while pursuing his prey.

The Beagle enjoys spending time with kids and other dogs, but will definitely take advantage of any chance to bother the household cat. These dogs are highly friendly and energetic, although they do have a tendency to pout if they don't get their way.

These dogs are indeed so sensitive that something as simple as hearing someone make fun of one of them after he has had an accident will make a Beagle brood for days. To prevent disturbing your dog's delicate sensitivities, you might need to caution your kids.

Beagles should learn at least the basics of obedience even when they occasionally become too focused on the pursuit to listen to directions.

27

You'll need to be persistent and patient when training your dog, so you might want to think about hiring a professional trainer by enrolling your pup in puppy obedience classes.

Beagles are omnivorous and enjoy eating. When put on a diet, a dog will gladly eat scraps. In fact, he might still reach for the trash cans for a post-dinner snack even if he is not on a diet.

To reduce shedding, your Beagle should be groomed once per week. Beagles often get enough exercise to wear their toenails down naturally, but you might want to examine your dog's nails to determine if they need to be cut at least once a month.

In general, beagles are a healthy breed. Some of these canines, though, are prone to epilepsy or cardiac problems. Of course, Beagles can also develop problems associated to obesity because of their inclination to overeat.

A Beagle can be the ideal dog for you if you're looking for a cheerful, well-behaved little friend.

28

Do You Want a Chow Chow as a Breed?

A blue-tongued dog would often be cause for alarm. However, it is entirely natural for your Chow Chow to have a blue tongue. The tongues of Chow Chows have a characteristic bluish tinge and are black.

The Chow Chow was developed in China as a hunting canine. These canines were introduced to England by Asian sailors, and their unusual appearance rapidly made them popular. The American Kennel Club classifies this breed as belonging to the Non-Sporting category.

The Chow Chow is a 17 to 20 inch tall, 45 to 70 pound dog. Because of its downward-curving lips, this breed can look to be agitated. The dog's thick double coat and curled-over tail counteract this aggressive appearance.

The most popular colour for Chow Chows is red, but they can also have black, blue, cream, cinnamon, or blue coats.

29

Although Chow Chows are not particularly energetic dogs, they do require a little more exercise than an apartment can offer. For this breed, a small fenced yard is sufficient.

Be ready to walk your Chow Chow every day if you do live in an apartment. However, keep in mind that Chows can be violent toward other dogs, so do not let him run loose in the park.

While Chow Chows are loyal to their families and typically enjoy spending time with kids, they frequently get along poorly with other pets.

In order to prevent their puppies from growing up to be hostile or harmful to outsiders, new owners should focus on socialising them.

A wonderful method to socialise your puppy and ensure that it receives extensive obedience training is to enrol it in puppy obedience lessons.

These dogs do have a few other problems in addition to their propensity to be distant and unpleasant toward individuals outside the household.

They have a propensity to bully inexperienced dog owners and to dominate humans if they can get away with it. You must be stern while dealing with your dog and make sure to always carry out orders.

30

Chows do not eat a lot because they are not very active dogs. When your dog is a puppy, you should feed him nutritious puppy food, and when he is an adult, you should feed him nutritious adult dog food.

Despite being simple to feed, they do need a lot of maintenance. Because they are so dense, it is difficult to brush their thick coats.

Despite being large dogs, Chow Chows should not be left outside for extended periods of time in the summer as their thick coats do not insulate them from heat sensitivity. Additionally susceptible to hip dysplasia, these dogs frequently experience issues with their knee joints.

Chow Chows may be the appropriate breed for you if you don't mind that they can be a bit of an attitude problem with people or other animals. On a freezing winter night, nothing compares to embracing one of these cuddly, bear-like pets.

Do You Want a Yorkshire Terrier?

A Yorkshire Terrier can be a good option for you if you appreciate small dogs with huge dog personalities.

31

These canines will take on a Great Dane without hesitation because they are so confident that they are just as large and bad as the opposition. It goes without saying that Yorkshire Terriers can still make excellent lap dogs. The Yorkie can snuggle just as well as anyone else.

The Toy Group of the American Kennel Club includes the Yorkshire Terrier. A Yorkie in the show ring appears to glide across the floor because its long, flowing coat conceals its tiny feet.

Despite the fact that Yorkies can weigh as little as one pound, the majority of breeders do not advise attempting to breed dogs this little, and for good reason.

Health is frequently neglected in favour of size and weight when dogs are raised to be this small. The Yorkie must weigh less than seven pounds, however the AKC does not specify a minimum weight.

The heads and legs of Yorkshire Terriers are tanned, and they have long, flowing coats of silver, blue, or black fur. All newborn Yorkie puppies are black and tan in hue. These dogs have dark, perceptive eyes.

The Yorkshire Terrier makes a great pet for apartments. Your Yorkie would undoubtedly like having a yard to run about in, but he can live without one. In fact, several Yorkshire Terriers never leave the house. Instead, these dogs have been litter-trained.

32

If you don't walk your Yorkie every day, try to find other methods to get him moving, such playing a game of fetch indoors. If you do have a yard, make sure the fence is completely enclosed because Yorkies like to explore.

Because Yorkshire Terriers are small and adorable, they don't usually have time to return home before a bystander brings the little dog home, believing it is lost or abandoned.

Since they are gregarious little dogs, Yorkshire Terriers love the commotion and action of family life. However, households with young children should avoid getting these dogs.

This is due to Yorkies' fragile nature and potential for injury, not because they are unreliable around young children. A well-behaved Yorkshire Terrier will allow children to pull, push, and prod him, but it is unfair to subject a young dog to such treatment.

Even though a Yorkie is a little dog, you should still enrol your pup in obedience training. Without enough instruction, these tiny fellas have a propensity to become obstinate and fixed in their ways. Additionally, if you can call your Yorkshire Terrier back to you if he escapes out the front door, obedience training can well save his life.

There aren't many major health issues with Yorkshire Terriers. They do frequently have dental issues, such baby teeth that haven't fallen out. Hernias and hypoglycemia are two other issues these tiny creatures may experience.

33

Your least expensive expense will probably be food for your Yorkshire Terrier. These tiny dogs don't consume much food. While dry food will help you keep your puppy's teeth in better shape, you must be careful not to spoil him with it or he may refuse to eat it.

To prevent matting, the majority of Yorkies should be groomed at least three times per week. Dogs with silkier coats might just require weekly grooming. Additionally, you should brush your dog's teeth multiple times a week because Yorkies are prone to dental issues.

A Yorkie can be the ideal breed for you if you're looking for a small dog with lots of spirit.

Do You Want a Boston Terrier?

Do you desire a canine companion that is as uniquely American as apple pie? If so, you might want to think about the Boston Terrier, one of the few breeds created in the United States.

These charming comedic characters first appeared in Boston in the 1800s.

34

The American Kennel Club recognised the Boston Terrier as the first American breed and included it in the Non Sporting Group. These canines range in size from 15 to 25 pounds and 15 to 17 inches.

These canines are extremely intelligent and have short muzzles and square skulls. Their short tails can be straight or corkscrewed, and their floppy jaws give them a slightly clownish appearance.

Brindle, seal, or black with white markings are all acceptable coat colours for Boston Terriers. A blaze of white between the eyes and white chest and front legs are symmetrical characteristics on the ideal Boston.

The Boston Terrier is a nice, amiable dog that hardly ever encounters a stranger it likes. Bostons enjoy spending time with their families because they receive a lot of attention and good snacks.

Although puppies may be too rough and rowdy for toddlers unless they are constantly watched, this breed truly enjoys kids. The Boston is renowned for its raucous and high-energy behaviour.

The intelligence of Boston Terriers makes learning enjoyable for them. Puppy classes are crucial for this breed since, in the absence of activities, your Boston will get into a lot of trouble.

When your Boston Terrier has mastered the fundamentals of obedience, you might wish to start entering him in agility and obedience competitions.

35

The majority of these dogs actually like taking part in these trials and relish the opportunity to perform for an audience.

The Boston Terrier may live happily in an apartment or tiny house despite its high energy level. You will need to take your dog for a long walk or a play session at the park every day if you don't have a fenced yard, though.

Don't be shocked if your dog is bouncing off the walls the next day if you cut his exercise routine short, especially if he is a young dog.

For many years, reckless breeders who didn't give a damn about breeding dogs with genetic issues put the Boston Terrier breed in grave risk of extinction.

Fanciers have saved this breed by putting a lot of effort and care into breeding. The breed still experiences a few typical health issues, though. These dogs are more prone to heart murmurs, cataracts, deafness, hypothyroidism, and damaged knees.

The immunological systems of many Bostons are also compromised, especially in infants younger than six months. This can result in a severe case of Demodectic mange, a disorder that causes bald areas and is not contagious.

Your dog may become entirely bald and infected with sores if they have a severe case of Demodectic mange. The majority of dogs recover from the ailment with therapy, but some never do and must be put to sleep after getting severe skin infections.

36

Despite being chowhounds, Boston Terriers do not consume nearly as much food as larger breeds.

These dogs burn through all of those calories quickly when they are young and active, but as they become older, you will need to pay special attention to your dog's weight. Consult your veterinarian about a diet for overweight dogs if he begins to put on weight around his chest.

You won't need to groom your Boston Terrier more than once a week unless he gets Demodectic mange. If it turns out that he does have mange, you will need to bathe him every day and frequently take him to the vet for extra care.

Some people find the Boston Terrier to be a bit overwhelming, but if you don't mind some noise and rowdy behaviour, let this dog's loving, affectionate temperament seduce you.

Does a Rottweiler Fit Your Personality?

Do you require a canine guardian that is knowledgeable and committed to its owners?

37

Then you might want to think about getting a Rottweiler. These large dogs were raised to be very adaptable working animals. They are excellent at agility training, guard their families and houses, and when they are with their owners, they treat them like miniature lapdogs.

The Rottweiler is a huge, powerful dog. These muscular dogs have a shoulder height of 22 to 27 inches and a weight range of 85 to 130 pounds. A Rottweiler features dark, soulful brown eyes and a sleek black and brown coat.

The Working Group of the American Kennel Club includes the Rottweiler. These strong canines are frequently employed as watchdogs.

Sadly, some Rottweiler owners have mistreated their animals in an effort to increase their level of aggression. These mistreated Rottweilers have unjustly earned the breed a bad name as a deadly breed. When bred and reared appropriately, rottweilers make fantastic, devoted family dogs.

It's not recommended to keep Rottweilers in apartments. These dogs require space to run because they are large and strong. Owners of Rottweilers should ideally live in a house with a fenced yard. You should be ready to frequently take your dog for runs in the park to burn off excess energy if you do not have a fenced yard.

The Rottweiler is a highly clever dog, and this breed thrives when given a task to complete.

38

You may make your Rottweiler happy by giving him a task, like keeping pests out of the garden. As Rottweiler puppies develop quickly into large, strong dogs, it's crucial to start training them early on.

Additionally, puppy lessons are a fantastic way for you to introduce your Rottweiler to a wide variety of social situations at an early age.

Fortunately, as long as the teacher is kind and patient, this breed enjoys learning. Because of their eagerness to take on new challenges, Rottweilers perform well in agility competitions.

Rottweilers might not be the ideal choice for a family with a child due to their size and strength. A six-month-old puppy might not be aware of his own strength and could inadvertently hurt young toddlers while playing. Wait until your kids are old enough to walk well if you have your heart set on a Rottweiler puppy.

A dog the size and energy of a Rottweiler will undoubtedly burn off a lot of calories. Be ready to spend a significant amount of money on food for your puppy. Additionally, it's critical to see to it that your puppy's nutritional requirements are being satisfied because Rottweilers are prone to developing joint issues as they age.

The short coat of a Rottweiler makes grooming them a relatively quick process. Slicker brushes should be used to groom your dog once a week to keep his coat looking healthy and glossy.

39

Make sure to check his nails as well to make sure they aren't too long. You could also want to get your dog used to having his teeth brushed while he is a puppy.

A Rottweiler might not be the breed for you if the prospect of a 100-pound dog trying to crawl into your lap as though he only weights ten pounds horrifies you. After all, not everyone wants a dog with a deadly exterior and a marshmallow heart.

You say you want a Dalmatian.

Given the appeal of the Disney animated films with dalmatians, it is understandable and amazing that this breed is popular. Although Dalmatian puppies can certainly cause trouble, much like their cartoon counterparts can, very few Dalmatians behave like the dogs in these films.

The American Kennel Club's Non-Sporting category includes the Dalmatian. During the 1700s, these dogs initially made their way to England, where noblemen employed them to protect their coaches.

40

Since they got along with horses, dalmatians were the perfect breed for the job. In fact, because firemen utilised horse-drawn fire trucks, Dalmatians were so wonderful with horses that they quickly gained popularity. Dalmatians and fire stations were intertwined by the time fire engines took the place of the horse-drawn wagon.

The Dalmatian weighs between 45 and 65 pounds and measures 19 to 24 inches tall. While not being unduly large or stocky, this dog has well-developed muscles. Brown, blue, or a blend of the two colours may be present in its eyes.

The long, beautiful tail of the Dalmatian is very strong. This breed's sleek coat has a white backdrop with black or brown patches all over it. Dalmatians do not have spots when they are young puppies. They are completely white before their spots start to show.

Due to their high level of energy, dalmatians are prone to hyperactivity and separation anxiety. Your dog may not be able to burn off all of his energy by himself when wandering around the yard, so be prepared to take him for a jog or a run in the park.

Give your Dalmatian a task if at all possible. No one has a horse in their backyard, but you can always train your dog to fetch the newspaper in the morning.

Due to their inclination to be a little stubborn, Dalmatians may not be suitable for inexperienced dog owners. If you purchase a Dalmatian puppy, be ready to go to puppy training sessions.

41

Additionally, socialise your puppy as often as you can because Dalmatians frequently exhibit apprehension around strangers.

Dalmatians burn a lot of calories due to their high level of activity. You must provide your puppy a high-quality, nutrient-dense puppy food. Additionally, ask your vet what vitamins and nutrients you should give your dog.

Additionally, since this breed is prone to kidney and bladder stones, find out about special diets that lessen the likelihood of them occurring. Among addition, allergies, hip dysplasia, and deafness are common in dalmatians.

A Dalmation is easy to groom. To get rid of loose hair, simply brush your dog once each week. Dalmations can be heavy shedders, so if you don't groom your dog, you'll spend a lot of time picking up his hair.

The Dalmation can be the ideal breed for you if you enjoy an active lifestyle and adore the beauty of the breed's spotty coat.

42

Does a Doberman Pinscher Fit Your Lifestyle?

In movies, Doberman Pinschers are frequently seen. Individuals are accustomed to witnessing people fleeing for their lives as vicious dogs rush at them while gazing menacingly into their eyes. But in reality, the majority of Dobermans make loving, knowledgeable household dogs.

The Doberman Pinscher is a member of the Working Group according to the American Kennel Club. Originally bred as police dogs, these dogs.

They were frequently employed by the German military as well. People were terrified as one of these large, frightening-looking dogs approached them. They are, after all, very strong creatures.

The Doberman Pinscher has a bullet-shaped skull, a muscular chest, and a square body. This breed reaches between 24 and 28 inches tall and weighs between 55 and 90 pounds. The Doberman has a short coat that is tan-marked and comes in black, red, blue, or fawn. These dogs occasionally have a white mark on their chests.

43

It has black eyes with an almond shape. The majority of Dobermans have docked tails. Although it may seem cruel, a docked tail can help avoid unpleasant mishaps in the future. Numerous undocked Dobermans have unintentionally damaged their tails.

Dobermans are not energetic dogs, yet they have incredible stamina. These dogs require exercise and do not adapt well to living in apartments. They would fit much better in a yard with fencing. Even if your yard is gated, you should be ready to walk your dog every day because Dobermans like spending time with their owners.

Despite the negative press this breed has received, most Dobermans get along well with kids and other animals. These loyal family dogs are very trainable and will stop at nothing to please their owners.

However, if you have young children and a Doberman puppy, you definitely need to exercise caution. Puppies can accidentally knock your kids down because they are so energetic and unaware of their own strength. As soon as you bring your Doberman home, you must start training and socialising him to prevent troublesome behaviours.

Dobermans are highly intelligent dogs that, if left alone, can cause quite a bit of trouble. Puppy obedience lessons are a fantastic choice since they will assist you in socialising and training your puppy while he is still a small puppy and easy to handle. Who wants to try teaching their dog to sit when he or she already weighs almost as much as they do?

44

Dobermans are large, powerful dogs who require a lot of dog food. To ensure that your dog receives the nutrition he needs, offer him a diet designed for large breeds.

Hypothyroidism and von Willebrand's disease are genetic conditions that can affect Doberman Pinschers. They may also experience heart issues. These large lap dogs are prone to gaining weight as they become older, so you might want to ask your vet about special meals for aged dogs.

A Doberman is simple to train. Your dog may only require a weekly brushing to get rid of dirt and loose hair, and you should examine his nails to make sure they aren't too long. Other than that, they seldom ever require any other maintenance.

Doberman Pinschers may appear to be cold-blooded assassins, but when it comes to their family, they are basically crème puffs. A Doberman can be the ideal breed for you if you want a dog that will guard your home but yet enjoying cuddling up next to you at night.

45

Do You Have the Right Breed in the Adorable Pug?

If you've seen Milo and Otis or Men In Black, you probably fell in love with the endearing Pugs who played the dogs in these films. While the Pug's unusual appearance may be what initially draws people to this breed, its disposition is what earns dog lovers' steadfast loyalty.

The Pug is categorised as belonging of the Toy Group by the American Kennel Club. Pugs typically weigh between 14 and 18 pounds. They have a slightly pig-like appearance thanks to their distinctively squished faces and curly tails.

Pugs have a black mask and can be silver, black, or beige in colour. Despite being little, they have wide chests and are highly muscular.

Pugs are known for having such a sweet disposition that people can practically tread on them. But don't be fooled by this breed's laid-back demeanour. If a stranger threatens his human, this dog will instantly go from a lover to a fighter. Pugs get along well with kids and other animals.

46

Pugs have also been known to achieve amazing feats like delicately bringing a lost parrot to its owner without ruffling a feather. Pugs, however, are more likely than some other breeds to trigger allergies. Children with asthma brought on by allergies shouldn't be around pugs.

Pugs are happy to live in townhouses or apartments. Even if the Pug doesn't need much activity, you need make sure he maintains his fitness to keep him healthy.

He should get enough exercise from daily strolls around the block, however he is also willing to walk much farther. Just make sure you put a harness on your Pug instead of a collar because these dogs already have pushed-in noses and don't need troubles with their windpipes.

Pugs are capable of learning obedience, but they take a while to pick things up. Your Pug could take longer than other breeds to learn how to sit or heel.

When he finds out, though, he will be incredibly proud of himself. Attending puppy obedience courses with your Pug could be something you want to try. If he simply cannot understand the commands, try again in a few months.

Pugs enjoy eating. If you give them sweets as a reward, they will learn disrespectful tricks and are delighted to eat whatever you give them.

47

Since Pugs are prone to knee issues that worsen if they are overweight, you should make every effort to restrict your dog's food intake. Pugs regularly sustain eye injuries and are susceptible to Demodectic mange.

A Pug is the best breed choice if you want a low-maintenance canine companion. Simply go over your dog's coat with a brush once a week to get rid of any loose hair and debris. Additionally, keep an eye on his facial lines to make sure they don't start to smell or grow bacteria.

A Pug can be the ideal breed for you if you want a canine that has heart and don't mind him snoring and snorting all night in your ear.

Considering the Saint Bernard

The hefty Saint Bernard saved the lives of numerous travellers who became lost in the cold Swiss Alps. This enormous dog was originally created by monks in the Alps to be a rescue dog. The Saint Bernard breed has a long history, dating back to the 1700s.

48

The Saint Bernard is assigned to the Working Group by the American Kennel Club. These large dogs are between 120 and 200 pounds in weight and are between 26 and 28 inches tall. This breed can have a coat that is long or short haired.

Since snow did not adhere to short hair very well in the beginning, all Saint Bernards had short hair. However, Saint Bernard enthusiasts bred them to have longer hair when these dogs were widely adopted as pets in Victorian England. They also made an effort to increase their size.

Sadly, some breeders today still place more value on outward looks than inner character. Before purchasing a puppy, confirm that the parents of your potential Saint Bernard are gregarious and patient animals.

Otherwise, you risk getting a scared or hostile dog. Do not undervalue the significance of selecting a puppy with a positive temperament.

Generally speaking, the Saint Bernard is a friendly giant who enjoys playing with kids and other dogs. Small children shouldn't be around young Saint Bernards, though, as these dogs tend to produce clumsy, ungainly puppies.

When attempting to play with a Saint Bernard puppy, more than one toddler has unintentionally fallen and suffered injuries. Older canines are typically more graceful and cautious around children.

49

Apartments and townhouses are not conducive to the Saint Bernard's well-being. These dogs require a lot of space and cannot be comfortable in a house without a fenced-in yard. Saint Bernards have a tendency to cause a lot of trouble if they do not get enough exercise. This large, bored dog may certainly cause a lot of harm.

Dogs with a great desire to please, Saint Bernards are devoted and caring companions. However, because of their great size, they can be challenging to manage.

While you still weigh more than your dog, you might want to think about signing him up for obedience lessons. In addition to helping you train him, these programmes are crucial for socialising your puppy. In the classes, he will encounter many strangers and their pets.

It is not surprising that feeding a Saint Bernard raises the grocery expenditure because they consume a lot of food.

Given that this breed is prone to hip dysplasia, you might wish to feed your puppy a meal designed to support the development of large breed puppies who are healthy and robust. Additionally, heart problems and malignancies are common in Saint Bernards.

Saint Bernards with short hair require relatively little care. Even dogs with long hair don't need a lot of labour because they aren't heavy objects. Just be sure to give your dog's coat a once-weekly brush.

50

The Saint Bernard makes a great companion animal. A Saint Bernard can be the ideal dog for you if you don't mind your dog being larger than most humans.

Does a Greyhound Fit Your Lifestyle?

Fast running is a sad trait of the greyhound breed. Many Greyhound owners train their dogs for racing and euthanize them after a string of defeats. These dogs can, however, also make fantastic pets, and many of them are given rehabilitation by Greyhound rescue organisations.

Before welcoming a lost Greyhound into your heart and home, you should consult the rescue about the challenges brand-new dog owners encounter. Greyhound racing dogs are taught to pursue an artificial rabbit. Sadly, they frequently fail to distinguish between a rabbit and a small dog or cat.

51

They thrive more as solitary pets. Additionally, although being fully grown, these dogs are not housebroken and are not potty trained.

The American Kennel Club classifies the Greyhound as belonging to the Hound Group. The earliest occurrence of these dogs was in ancient Egypt, where they were employed to pursue prey.

When they arrived in England, they were widely used by British nobility, who then started racing them. The owners of the greyhounds who migrated to America carried on this well-liked sport.

Large and strongly built canines, greyhounds are. They have slim bodies and lengthy legs. All of these dogs have muscle. Greyhounds have long, beautiful tails and dark eyes. Greyhounds, unlike many other breeds, can be any colour.

Although they can reach tremendous speeds, greyhounds are not typically high energy canines. These canines are couch potatoes in between races, saving their energy for the next chase.

Although dogs that live in apartments often have little trouble adjusting to walking on a leash, they do need a fenced yard so they have space to run.

Greyhounds are social, amiable canines. They are highly playful and like spending time with their family. Nothing pleases them more than spending the entire evening curled up next to their owners on the couch.

52

Children can play with greyhounds, and they are treated gently. They enjoy playing with other dogs as well. If you have other pets, you'll need to keep a careful check on your dog because the predatory drive might be too strong to overcome.

Greyhounds' bodies require a lot of fuel. You'll need to provide your dog premium dog food. Don't let your dog overeat, though, as these dogs are prone to bloating. His health is better off eating several small meals as opposed to one huge one.

To determine how much you should feed your dog at each meal, speak with your veterinarian. For these dogs, a quality vitamin supplement is also a smart option.

Greyhounds have a short, smooth coat that sheds minimally, making grooming them easy. You only need to brush your Greyhound once a week. If his nails are scraping the floor while he walks, you might also wish to clip them.

At first, having one of these canines can be daunting. However, if you are persistent, you may acquire a lovely, dedicated family pet who will remain with you for a very long time.

53

Is a Jack Russell Terrier a Good Investment?

Jack Russell Terriers are spirited, active canines that became well-known after the Wishbone television series debuted. These dogs are not exactly like the well-known Wishbone in real life, though. All Jack Russells are terriers, thus for novice dog owners, the breed's disposition can occasionally be overwhelming.

Because Reverend Jack Russell, a parson, developed the Jack Russell Terrier breed, it is also known as the Parson Russell Terrier. He raised these dogs specifically to hunt foxes. He kept the dogs small because he wanted them to be able to fit into the area where the fox was hiding.

The Terrier Group of the American Kennel Club includes the Jack Russell Terrier. To distinguish these dogs from British Jack Russells, the AKC refers to them as Parson's Russell Terriers. This is important because British breeders favour dogs with shorter legs but the AKC believes that these dogs should have long legs.

Small but mighty, Jack Russell terriers are dogs. Their brown almond-shaped eyes appear attentive and bright-eyed.

Although the majority of Jack Russells have short coats, some have rougher coats. Always more than half white, these dogs. Their body's remaining areas are marked with a mixture of tan, black, and brown marks.

The Jack Russell Terrier's short tail is carried straight up and is rarely still since this breed is nearly never without an eager tail wag. These dogs are 10 to 15 inches height and weigh 13 to 17 pounds.

The Jack Russell Terrier is a canine with a lot of energy. Despite its little size, this dog fares poorly in flats or other compact areas. This dog will keep working until it breaks because it perceives itself as much larger than it actually is.

A Jack Russell needs a yard that is completely fenced. When bored, Jack Russells will navigate around, under, and over barriers to find a way out. Even trees are not beyond them.

As long as they aren't forgotten in the flurry of family life, Jack Russells appreciate living in the middle of a busy household. They enjoy playing games with kids, such as chasing and retrieving balls, and enjoy receiving plenty of attention.

The diminutive size of the Jack Russell should not cause you to overlook obedience training. The framework that commands offer is necessary for these dogs. You can socialise your puppy in puppy lessons so that he learns how to play well with other dogs.

<h2 style="text-align:center">55</h2>

Deafness, as well as sight and ear issues, can affect Jack Russells. This breed is generally healthy, nevertheless.

Due to their small appetites, Jack Russells are not very expensive to feed. But if your dog starts acting hyper, you might want to talk to your vet about switching to a lower-protein diet.

Jack Russells with smooth coats require relatively little care. Dogs with coarse coats, however, need to be groomed at least once a week. Check your dog's nails frequently to make sure they aren't getting too long.

A Jack Russell can be entertaining for the family. The Jack Russell might be the ideal breed for you, provided that your family doesn't include many couch potatoes.

56

You'd Like a Standard Poodle, Right?

Some people dismiss the fluffy, perfectly coiffed Standard Poodles in the show ring as foolish, superficial dogs after taking one glance at them. The Standard Poodle, on the other hand, is regarded by many as the most intelligent breed in the world, having the mental capacity of a three-year-old kid.

Despite their appearance in the show ring, these dogs were initially bred to work hard in the water. The Standard Poodle spent hours retrieving waterfowl for hunters, keeping itself warm and dry because to the breed's thick coat.

The Standard Poodle is categorised in the Non-Sporting Group by The American Kennel Club because it is no longer frequently used as a working dog. These dogs are over 15 inches tall and range in weight from 45 to 70 pounds.

57

Under all of that hair, the Standard Poodle has a robust body. It has long, folded ears that are located close to the head, and its intelligent, dark-brown eyes. This dog has an upright, docked tail. The dog's tail shouldn't slant over its back.

The Standard Poodle is available in a variety of hues, including parti-colored, apricot, black, cream, red, blue, grey, silver, and white.

Overall, black Standard Poodles appear to be calmer than other hues, whereas white and cream Standard Poodles appear to be slightly more anxious.

The Standard Poodle thrives in a family environment and is incredibly dedicated to the youngsters in the household. The Standard Poodle rarely encounters a dog it doesn't like, making it a great breed choice for households with multiple dogs.

If you have a cat, be prepared for your dog to run amok while pursuing it through the house; but, once he catches up to the cat, he will only want to play.

Your dog needs to go for a long walk or play in the park every day if you live in an apartment. These dogs can live in apartments, but a house with a fenced yard is much preferable for them.

This breed, which is highly intelligent, enjoys learning and ought to take puppy obedience training. Additionally, Standard Poodles must be taught from an early age to avoid having their inherent reserve toward strangers develop into fear.

58

Your puppy will put forth a lot of effort in class because he wants to earn your favour. He will furrow his brow and attempt again if he is unable to understand what you want him to do. If he's still stumped, he can start to feel down and frustrated.

If this occurs, offer him a familiar command, and when he joyfully complies, he will be prepared to try to learn the unfamiliar instruction once more. In order to participate in obedience and agility competitions, many Standard Poodles and their owners continue their education by taking advanced classes.

There are a number of prevalent health issues in the Standard Poodle breed. Due to the high prevalence of Addison's disease, hip dysplasia, and epilepsy issues, many breeders actually check their parent dogs to ensure they are free of these genetic defects. Additionally, your dog could get skin issues, bloat, and renal failure.

The standard poodle is a large dog with a large appetite. Be ready for a substantial rise in the grocery expenditure if you've never had a large dog before. These pets should also get a vitamin every day. Additionally, find out from your vet if feeding your poodle a daily vitamin C tablet will help reduce the risk of hip dysplasia, according to numerous vets.

Don't get a Standard Poodle if you don't want to spend time grooming a dog. These dogs require daily brushing, which can take an hour or more due to their big size and the length of time it takes to completely brush out a Standard Poodle's coat.

59

A professional groomer will need to take care of your poodle's hair every six weeks, therefore you will need to learn how to do it yourself.

The Standard Poodle is a playful, smart dog. This breed might be right for you if you don't mind brushing your dog instead of watching the news.

Is Buying a Newfoundland a Good Idea?

You might want to purchase a Newfoundland if you're searching for a family dog who will dedicate his life to keeping your kids out of mischief.

These enormous canines are extraordinarily kind and sensitive, and they have a natural impulse to save people who are in danger. To be sure you can take care of such a big dog, you need think about it before purchasing a Newfoundland puppy.

The Newfoundland weighs between 100 and 150 pounds and is a big, sturdy dog. The shoulder height of these gentle giants ranges from 26 to 28 inches.

60

The waterproof double coat of a Newfoundland can be black, brown, grey, or black and white. The majority of dogs have dark chocolate brown eyes, however few do have lighter brown eyes.

Newfoundlands are regarded by the American Kennel Club as being a component of the Working Group. These dogs were frequently kept by lighthouse keepers and were excellent in rescue scenarios.

They are the ideal dog breed to assist in sea rescues because to their huge size, thick, water-resistant double coat, and water resistance.

The Newfoundland is a poor fit for small-roomed apartments and houses due of its enormous size. These dogs don't have high anxiety levels and don't require a lot of activity.

Usually, a fence around the yard is enough. Of course, they still take their owners on leisurely nighttime strolls.

For a Newfoundland to be regarded as a representative of the breed, they must have a wonderful disposition. These dogs must be trained as puppies not to jump up due to their great size in order to prevent them from knocking children over.

However, they typically take great care to avoid hurting children or animals and appear to grasp instinctively how delicate they are.

When a youngster or another dog wants to play, Newfoundlands will sit regally and observe their surroundings. They will therefore gladly forfeit their dignity in order to play with their friends.

61

Newfoundlands should be trained in obedience as puppies due to their size. Although they like delighting their owners, training a six-month-old Newfoundland can be difficult due to their size and strength. Puppy obedience should be fun for these canines because they enjoy learning and playing with the other puppies in the class.

Any dog that weighs more than 100 pounds consumes a lot of food, so if you purchase a Newfoundland, be ready for an increase in your grocery cost. Be sure to discuss your puppy's dietary requirements with your veterinarian because huge dogs like these need the correct vitamins and other nutrients to build strong bones.

Despite the breed's long hair, taking care of a Newfoundland doesn't take much time. The top coat's coarse hair does not mat easily. You should be able to keep your dog's coat looking excellent as long as you can set aside time to brush him at least once each week.

Ensure that his nails are not in need of trimming by checking them at least once a month.

A Newfoundland might not be the breed for you if you can't envisage owning a dog the size of a miniature pony. But if you don't mind this breed's big size, you'll have a devoted and obedient friend for years to come.

62

Is Buying a Miniature Pinscher a Good Idea?

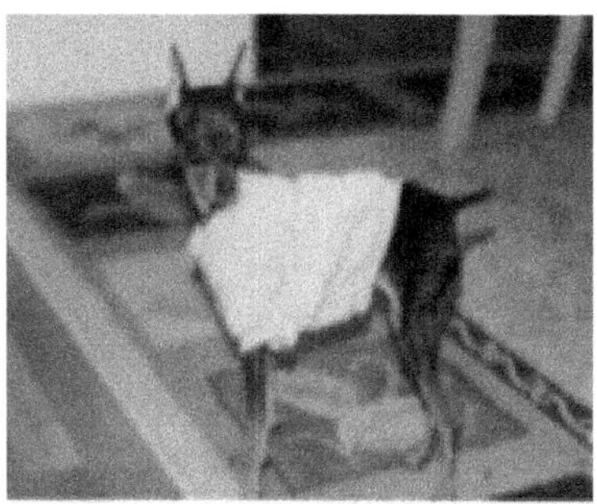

If you adore the Doberman Pinscher's lean, muscular appearance but don't want a large dog, you might want to think about getting a Miniature Pinscher. These canines look a lot like Dobermans, yet they weigh almost a hundred pounds less.

Although the Miniature Pinscher resembles a Doberman in size, they are not genetically related. In actuality, the Miniature Pinscher predates the Doberman in development.

By crossing the German Pinscher with a smaller breed, the Miniature Pinscher was developed. The Miniature Pinscher is a member of the Toy Group according to the American Kennel Club, however these dogs are not small, cuddly lapdogs.

The Miniature Pinscher was developed as a hardy, domineering ratter. The Min Pin stands 10 to 12 inches tall and weighs 8 to 10 pounds.

63

The physique of little Pinschers is small and powerful. Their sharp eyes are a deep brown that almost appear black. Short coats of Min Pins come in red, stag red, black and rust, or chocolate and rust. The tails of this breed are docked.

Some owners also crop the ears of their Miniature Pinschers, but this is not necessary. As these canines become older, the majority of them get pricked ears.

If you are ready to take your high activity Miniature Pinscher for a long walk once a day, they do well in apartments. Of course, the independence of a fenced yard is also enjoyable to the Min Pin.

Make sure your yard has a securely enclosed exercise area because these dogs like to roam and will look for ways to get out. Your dog escaping could be fatal if you reside in a neighbourhood with busy streets because Miniature Pinschers can't be easily noticed from moving cars.

Although miniature pinschers are extremely devoted to their owners and loyal pets, their loyalty does not often extend to young children. With infants and young children, this breed has a propensity to be aggressive.

You might wish to kennel your dog while your guests are here if you frequently have visiting family members with young children in order to prevent issues. Additionally, some of these dogs are highly tense and will bite adults, particularly mailmen and deliverymen.

64

Although Miniature Pinschers are little, the majority of them are somewhat independent and challenging to train. You should be careful to obey every command, and your puppy should take obedience training.

These dogs enjoy practising agility, and competing allows them to show off. The Min Pin was developed as a working dog and is wary of rodents. Your dog won't sleep until the mouse is caught if one manages to get inside your home.

Numerous severe medical disorders, including thyroid, heart, and epileptic conditions, can affect miniature pinschers. Additionally, these dogs are susceptible to hip dysplasia, a condition that is uncommon in petite breeds.

Despite their inclination to be a little gluttonous, little Pinschers do not eat a lot of food. If you find that your elegant Miniature Pinscher is beginning to take on the appearance of a blowfish with legs, you might need to switch to a food that prevents weight growth.

Although Min Pins don't need much care, they do struggle with growing nails. Make sure to regularly inspect your dog's nails.

The Miniature Pinscher is not for everyone, but if you want a canine companion who will be utterly devoted to you, you might want to give it some thought.

65

Do You Fit the Siberian Husky Ideal?

Are you seeking for a dog that enjoys people's company but is also incredibly active? If so, you might want to think about getting a Siberian husky. This gorgeous canine was developed to toil endlessly pulling sleds loaded with supplies over kilometres of snowy terrain. Huskies give their owners companionship at the end of the day.

The American Kennel Club categorises the Siberian Husky as a member of the Working Group. The Husky must have a task to complete, like the majority of dogs in this pack, to prevent him from getting into mischief.

These dogs are more wolf-like and less domesticated than many other dog breeds. The Husky is a twenty- to twenty-four-inch-tall, thirty-five to sixty-pound dog.

These energetic dogs have a thick, two-layer coat that is highly dense. Huskies have wolf-like features, including prickly ears. Although there are many different colours for this breed, most Huskies have black and white or silver and white coats.

66

The Husky's almond-shaped blue or brown eyes are his most distinguishing characteristic.

Being a very impulsive dog, the Siberian Husky is more likely than nearly any other breed to get into accidents and dangerous situations. Routinely, more than one Husky comes in for repairs at the vet's office.

Although these dogs typically get along well with older kids, they might not be the greatest choice for families with young children. Huskies are known for being aggressive toward cats or other small animals, so they might not be a good choice for families with young children.

Due to its high level of energy, the Husky does not adapt well to small yards or apartments. In fact, because of their thick coats, Huskies prefer to spend the majority of the colder months outside because interior temperatures are uncomfortable for them.

Just make sure your yard is well fenced in because these dogs have a tendency to pull Houdini-like escapes.

Given that the Siberian Husky is continuously on the lookout for indicators of weakness, it is crucial that you train your dog carefully. If you want some assistance teaching your puppy, you might wish to take him to obedience courses.

67

Your dog will become a nightmare to own if you do not maintain a dominant posture. Huskies are best suited to knowledgeable dog owners.

Siberian Huskies have a large appetite, however some of these dogs may not eat well when they are tense or anxious. Naturally, other Huskies devour everything, even the siding of the houses.

To remove dirt and debris, Siberian Huskies should be groomed once each week. Of course, you might want to groom your dog more frequently when he is shedding his coat.

Huskies are generally in good health. The majority of husky health issues are accident-related, while hip dysplasia and hypothyroidism are also possible in this breed.

Consider getting a gorgeous Siberian Husky if you don't mind having a dog who continuously keeps you on your toes.

68

Must You Purchase a Bloodhound?

Films about escaped prisoners frequently feature the Bloodhound. To an escapee, the sound of these large canines baying as they locate the smell they are looking for may be frightening, but it may also be soothing. After all, Bloodhounds are used to find lost or confused individuals.

The Bloodhound, a dog belonging to the hound group of the American Kennel Club, is between twenty-three and twenty-seven inches tall and between eighty and one hundred ten pounds in weight.

These canines are distinguished by their long, drooping ears and dismal, wrinkled looks. They have coarse, short coats that can be either black and tan, red, or liver and tan in hue.

Bloodhounds are too affectionate to be utilised as guard or attack dogs, despite the fact that criminals are afraid of them. A Bloodhound will locate a man's smell, it's true, but these canines don't go hunting to hurt humans.

Bloodhounds must be trained by handlers because they will approach a seasoned killer like a long-lost friend and run up to him.

Although these canines are excellent for families because of their loving demeanour, Bloodhounds do have a few peculiarities.

Because this breed is a decision maker, obedience training does not work well with it. The Bloodhound is less likely to listen to commands and is more stubborn than most other breeds due to the same characteristics that allow this breed to follow down scents.

There is a lot of patience and understanding involved in training your Bloodhound to comply. Never yell at him or treat him rudely because doing so could leave a permanent scar.

If you are having trouble training your dog to heed orders, you might want to think about hiring a professional dog trainer who use positive reinforcement techniques.

The Bloodhound enjoys spending time with its family, however it is impossible for this breed to live in a city. Compared to most breeds, bloodhounds require greater exercise. The ideal home has a sizable fenced yard. To burn off surplus energy, you might also need to take your Bloodhound for lengthy walks.

70

Bloodhounds like to eat and can significantly alter your grocery budget. You might want to speak with your veterinarian to determine whether you should feed your Bloodhound a special brand of dog food because these dogs are prone to hip dysplasia and stomach issues.

Although Bloodhounds don't require frequent brushing, it is nevertheless necessary to clean their facial creases and wrinkles to stop the growth of bacteria and odours. If adequate air does not reach your dog's ears, you should also be ready for him to get an ear infection.

Every breed that has existed since long before the Dark Ages has some health issues. In addition to hip dysplasia and gastrointestinal issues, the Bloodhound can experience eyelid issues.

The Bloodhound's most annoying issue, meanwhile, is not an illness. The Bloodhound drools and slobbers more than most other breeds due to its droopy lips, which add to its melancholy aspect.

Take a hard look at the Bloodhound if you want a breed of dog that has endured the test of time and still has a lovely disposition.

71

You say you want a Bichon Frise.

If you have allergies and yet want a dog, you might want to look into the Bichon Frise breed. This adorable tiny dog's primary purpose in life is to be a buddy, and it excels at it.

The American Kennel Club categorises the Bichon Frise as belonging to the Non-Sporting Group. The Bichon is a small dog that weighs seven to thirteen pounds and is nine to eleven inches tall.

These adorable small dogs are distinguished by their thick white coats and bright, attentive eyes. The tail of the Bichon is displayed proudly over its back.

As long as the kids are old enough to understand how to handle a dog without hurting it, bichons make the ideal family pet. Although your Bichon may put up with hard handling, he is prone to injury. These dogs get along well with other dogs and animals, including older kids.

72

The Bichon Frise enjoys social interactions and is quite satisfied to live in an apartment or townhouse. Your dog won't object to a house with a fenced yard, of course.

In order to keep your dog strong and healthy if you don't have a fenced yard, you should be ready to take him for a daily walk around the block.

Despite the fact that Bichon Frises are small dogs without a tendency to be rebellious, it is nevertheless advisable to teach your puppy some fundamental obedience commands.

You'll want to make sure that you can call your Bichon back to your side if he ever darts out the front door and toward the street. Of course, you can instruct him in a few basic instructions on your own, but puppy obedience classes can facilitate learning.

Additionally, you may teach your puppy socialising skills through these sessions. Of course, if you start taking classes in obedience, your child's propensity for compliance might simply persuade you to keep learning.

These canines are reputed to be extremely intelligent. In actuality, Bichons frequently appear as expertly trained circus dogs.

Feeding a Bichon Frise is not expensive. Small dogs frequently experience dental issues, therefore you might wish to utilise a dry food diet. Make sure to regularly brush your puppy's teeth if you choose to offer him soft food.

73

The Bichon Frise breed's one flaw is that these canines require intensive grooming. If you don't regularly brush your Bichon's fluffy coat, he'll end up looking like a nasty mop head rather than a charming, refined little dog.

Additionally, you will need to get his coat styled and cropped at least once every month. This can turn into a significant investment if you can't groom your dog yourself.

The good news is that the breed of Bichon Frise is highly healthy. In actuality, this breed has no typical health issues.

A Bichon Frise can be the ideal dog breed for you and your family if you want a cuddly, affectionate pet that won't make you break out in hives.

You'd want a Bull Terrier, then

Despite being a good dog, the Bull Terrier has a negative image. This dog was bred to fight, and when a Bull Terrier is mistreated, that aggression and even viciousness can develop.

74

A Bull Terrier puppy can develop into a caring and affectionate adult dog with the right care and training. In some instances, this breed can even be a little foolish.

However, an older dog who has experienced abuse might never be completely trustworthy and shouldn't be kept in a household with kids.

The American Kennel Club's terrier group includes the Bull Terrier, which is typically pure white or brindled in colour. However, white markings cannot be the predominate colour on brindle canines.

This dog should not be confused with its cousin, the American Pit Bull Terrier. The Bull Terrier weighs between 55 and 70 pounds and is a robust, muscular dog. The breed's unique defining features are the dog's broad chest and bullet-shaped head.

When given plenty of exercise, the Bull Terrier is content to live in an apartment. However, these dogs favour being in a house with a sizable yard that is completely fenced in.

Make sure your dog cannot escape wherever or however you exercise him because some Bull Terriers and cats or small dogs can make a lethal combination.

Bull Terriers adore their families and frequently get along well with kids. These dogs like playing and will play frisbee for hours.

75

Never leave your Bull Terrier alone with young children who are visiting, though, if you don't have your own kids and they aren't used to them. Young children can often be mistaken for other animals rather than people.

The Bull Terrier is most definitely not the breed for someone who has never owned a dog. These canines don't work well with novice dog owners.

Additionally, your Bull Terrier will detect it if you are a timid person as opposed to an authoritative person. He'll take control of your home and quickly overpower you.

You must make sure that your dog is fully taught before he grows too big for you to simply control because Bull Terriers are such strong animals.

Enrolling your dog in puppy obedience classes will ensure that he receives the proper training while still a young puppy. Obedience training sessions are also a crucial part of socialising your dog.

Bull Terriers are able to consume a lot of dog food. These dogs can have a significant impact on the grocery budget even if they don't consume as much food as a Great Dane.

You might want to talk to your vet about giving your Bull Terrier a kidney-friendly dog food. The Bull Terrier is susceptible to kidney illness as well as heart disease and hearing loss.

76

Very little grooming is necessary for your Bull Terrier. To keep his coat appearing smooth and healthy, you might wish to brush him once a week to get rid of stray hair and debris. You might also want to give him a tooth brushing and cut his nails.

If you have experience with dog ownership and are prepared to train your dog to be a good citizen, you might want to consider the Bull Terrier.

Do You Want to Buy a Chihuahua?

If you watch television, you've probably seen famous people carrying around little puppies with large poppy brown eyes, like Paris Hilton.

One of the tiniest dog breeds in the world is this one, the Chihuahua. Chihuahuas thrive in warmer climates and made their debut in Mexico. Naturally, a dog sweater can keep one of these tiny canines warm and comfortable during the winter.

77

The Chihuahua is a small dog that weighs between one and six pounds and is only five inches tall. Although there are many different colours available for these tiny pups, tans or black and tans are the most popular.

Their large, somewhat poppy eyes are accompanied by prickly ears and an alert attitude. Both short and long haired variations of this breed exist.

Chihuahuas are regarded by the American Kennel Club as belonging to the Toy Group. These dogs are excellent companion animals because they were bred to be them. This breed prefers to be involved in the action and despises alone.

Due to their small size and lack of exercise requirements, chihuahuas are excellent apartment dogs. These little fellows can even be taught to use a litter box by some people. This does not imply, however, that a Chihuahua won't like residing in a home with a yard. On warm days, this breed enjoys playing and exercising outside.

Small children should be kept away from the Chihuahua since it occasionally bites them, especially if it has just had an injury and feels threatened by their presence.

Additionally, this breed is prone to becoming domineering and easily spoilt, especially if its owners give it free rein to act aggressively or angrily.

78

You must make sure that your Chihuahua does not bully your other pets if you have any. These canines, who really believe they possess the size and strength of a Rottweiler, will engage in combat with much larger dogs. In fact, the Chihuahua makes a great security dog and is willing to fight off invaders who are human.

Chihuahuas need puppy obedience training since they often act poorly and are self-centered. After all, it can be unpleasant to be around a small dictator.

Puppy lessons will assist in your dog learning the fundamentals of obedience, but they also serve the vital function of socialising your new puppy.

Early on, he will learn how to get along with both people and other dogs. These dogs are highly bright and respond well to obedience instruction despite their size. Even after that, some of them enrol in agility training.

Even while chihuahuas consume very little food, their fussy eating habits might make feeding them expensive. Some dogs in this breed have difficulty eating dry, hard food because they are so delicate. Chihuahuas are prone to rheumatism, epilepsy, fractures, and dislocated jaws.

Chihuahuas with short hair require relatively little maintenance. Long-haired Chihuahuas require a little bit more grooming, but they still just require weekly brushing.

79

You may also want to brush your dog's teeth every day because some of these dogs have dental issues due to their small jaws.

A Chihuahua can be the appropriate dog for you if you desire a canine companion who is small enough to fit in your pocket but has the heart of a much larger dog.

Conclusion

There are many different types of dogs, each with their own unique set of characteristics. When choosing a dog, it is important to consider which breed would be the best fit for your lifestyle and personality.

Some breeds are better suited for active families, while others are more laid back and content to lounge around the house. There are also breeds that are better suited for living in apartments, and those that do best in rural environments. With so many different breeds to choose from, there is sure to be a perfect match for everyone.

I hope you enjoyed reading this short book as much as I enjoyed writing it.

God Bless!

Troy Ludo

80

Don't miss out!

Visit the website below and you can sign up to receive emails whenever Troy Ludo publishes a new book. There's no charge and no obligation.

https://books2read.com/r/B-A-NWCV-ZVWDC

Connecting independent readers to independent writers.

Also by Troy Ludo

Aquarium Care Made Simple
How To Lose Weight: And Stay In Shape Permanently
Easy Self Improvement: The Ultimate Guide
Dog Breeds: Profiles of Popular Dog Breeds and Buying Advice
Single Parenting: Become Your Child's Best Parent!

About the Author

Troy Ludo is an author, researcher, and business owner. He enjoys discovering new topics of interest, and sharing his findings with the world through writing.